MÜNCHEN *life*

Das seltsame Leben und Treiben
im Millionendorf München
fotografiert von
HEINZ GEBHARDT
und mit Worten näher erklärt von
KARL WANNINGER

The Strange Life and Customs
of München, Bavaria's Village Metropolis
Photography by
HEINZ GEBHARDT
Commentary by
KARL WANNINGER

Bruckmann München

München leuchtet und strahlt nicht mehr:
München dröhnt im Verkehr, spricht in
allen Sprachen der Welt, macht Karriere als
Olympiastadt und wird von ihren Bewoh-
nern Weltstadt genannt – aber Weltstadt mit
Herz.
München besteht nicht mehr aus einem
weißblauen Föhnhimmel mit malerischen
Hausfassaden im goldenen Abendlicht,
sondern aus 1 364 920 Menschen, die in
Wohnsilos, Zehnquadratmeterzimmern
und Eigentumswohnungen leben, den
Föhn verfluchen wegen der Kopfschmerzen
und die wenigen malerischen Häuser meist
nur von außen kennen, denn innen tickt
ein Computer…
München, das sind heute 1 364 920 Leute,
die ihre Stadt mit Bagger und Beton neu
gebaut haben, ihr olympische Ringe um
den Hals legten, aber dabei nie vergessen
haben, wozu sie ihre Stadt brauchen:
zum Leben.
Und die Münchner leben!
Von den Pennern am Rindermarktbrunnen
bis zu den Millionärssöhnen, umflattert
von Schmetterlingen, die angeblich nicht
weinen…
Von chrysanthemenbeflaggten Jünglingen
die ihrer Debütantin das eiskalte Händ-
chen küssen, bis zu dem Typ, der dem
anderen Typ einen Trip einwirft…
Von Hot-pants-Sekretärinnen, Briefträgern
Oberinspektoren bis zu den Einbrechern,
Hochstaplern, Zuhältern – sie alle leben
gern in Deutschlands heimlicher Haupt-
stadt:
So zwischen orientaler Gleichgültigkeit
und business – immer umweht von Künst-
lern, Sternchen und Halbpoeten, von
großen und kleinen Namen –
eingegiftet vom täglichen Verkehrschaos –
erschreckt vom Verbrechen –
und immer wieder versöhnt von der Gewiß-
heit, an einem Punkt der Erde zu sitzen, an
dem wie an keinem anderen ein Wort ganz
groß geschrieben wird: »Leben…«

No longer tranquil and radiant as in days of yore, modern München pulsates with traffic and the air is full of snatches of conversation in many tongues: it has embarked upon its career as an Olympic City.

München no longer consists of a white and blue sky, indicating the presence of the fall wind from the Alps, or picturesque houses with frescoed fronts which glow in the evening sun, but of a massive population of 1,364,920 human beings living in tiny flats, in enormous tenement blocks or in privately owned penthouses, who curse the fall wind for giving them a headache and know the isolated picturesque houses only from passing, for within their four walls a computer is ticking away ...

München's present population of 1,364,920 built their city from scratch with bulldozers and a million tons of ferroconcrete. Although they have shouldered the responsibility of the Olympic venture, they never forget that their city is primarily intended as a place to live in.

And how they enjoy it!

From the tramps that collect around the Rindermarkt fountain to the scions of the wealthy, fluttered around by the kind of butterflies that, it is said, never shed a tear...

from the young sparks with chrysanthemum-buttonholes kissing the ice-cold hand of a deb to the hippie who sends another hippie off on a trip...

from typists in hot-pants, mailmen, police officers to burglars, con men, pimps—all enjoy life in West Germany's "underground capital."

Half-way between oriental unflappability and keen business sense—invariably surrounded by a bevy of artists, starlets and would-be poets,

celebrities, major and minor—

stuck in daily traffic jams—

shocked by sensational headlines—

yet constantly reassured by the fact of living in a place where one word looms larger than all others: "Life ..."

(die Leute in München)

The ways of München folk

d' Leit

Die Schutzleute dirigieren – die Menschen folgen nicht.
Die Gaffer gaffen, staunen, betrachten, grinsen, spotten,
sind noch biedermeierisch veranlagt und wollen sich nicht
an den Großstadtbetrieb gewöhnen.
Die Automobile hupen – die Radfahrer warten – die Hunde
stören – die Tauben fliegen – die Straßenbahnen kommen
daher und fahren dahin – das Pflaster wird betreten – die
Inseln ebenfalls – die Wasserpfützen auch ebenfalls – die
Bogenlampen brennen (nachts) – die Zigarrenstumpen
liegen – die weggeworfenen Trambahnfahrscheine flattern –

Traffic policemen direct the traffic – the pedestrians couldn't
care less. Yokels stare open-mouthed, flabbergasted, or
crack jokes. Out of step with their time, they cannot adapt to
the pace of life in a big city.
Cars hoot – cyclists wait – dogs tie up the traffic – pigeons
take off in a bunch – streetcars approach and pass by –
people disregard danger signs, collect at streetcar stops,
hop through puddles – luminaires light up the street at
night – cigarette butts lie scattered around – used streetcar
tickets flutter in the wind –

der Benzingestank ist tagtäglich und
somit der ganze Zustand unerträglich!
Karl Valentin 1930

day in, day out the constant stench of
gasoline poisons the air, the whole
situation is intolerable.
Karl Valentin 1930

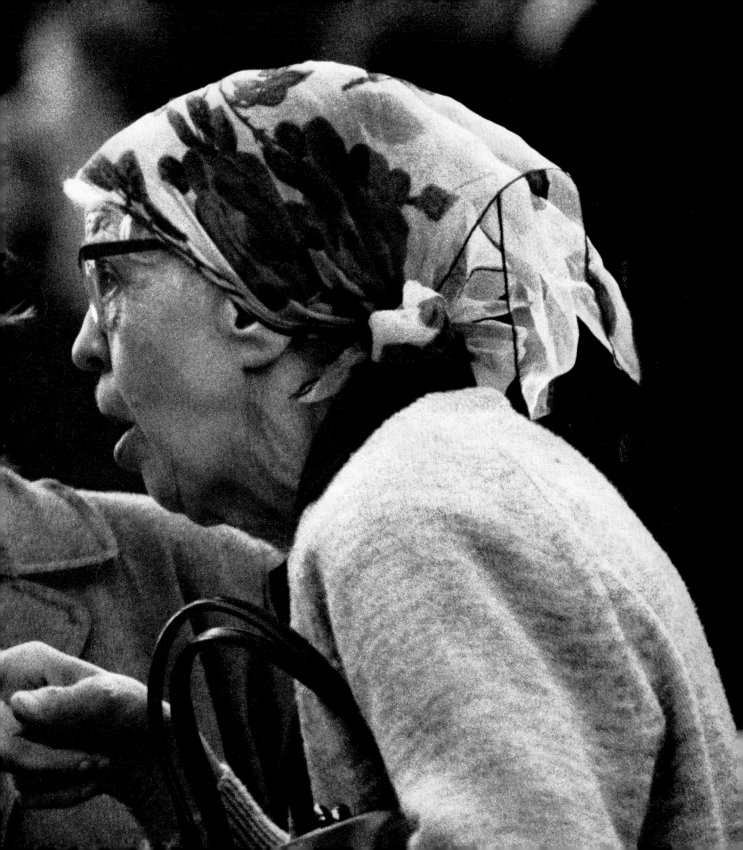

Der Münchner *Frühling Springtime*
bringt die Auer Dult, in München brings out the Auer Dult and
die Mädchen und die Gefühle. its antiques, girls and spring feelings.

Das »deutsche Fräuleinwunder«
entdeckten die Amerikaner in
München. Die wadlstrumpf-
bewaffnete Bergsteigerdirn von
einst ist längst ausgestorben.
Die Münchnerin der 70er Jahre
hat Weltstadtformat, und bevor
sich um 18.35 Uhr die Kaufhaus-
tore schließen, strömen
sie heraus: die Jungen, die Schö-
nen und die Eleganten.
König Ludwig I. von Bayern
ließ vor 150 Jahren eine Schön-
heitsgalerie malen mit Lola Montez und den schönsten Bürgers-
töchtern. Heute hätte er die Qual
der Wahl…

It was in München the Americans
discovered what they called the
"German Fräulein Miracle." The
race of clodhopping country
wenches of byegone days is long
extinct. München's fräuleins of
the 'seventies compare in chic
with those of any other great
city, and before the department
stores close at 18.35, they
stream out through the exits:
the young, the beautiful, the
elegant.
A hundred and fifty years ago
Bavaria's first King Ludwig collected a Beauty Gallery with
portrait paintings of Lola Montez
and the most beautiful daugh-
ters of his commoner subjects.
Nowadays he would have
experienced great difficulty in
making his choice…

Münchner Philharmoniker	212 Musiker
Rundfunkorchester	75 Musiker
Staatsoper	147 Musiker
Gärtnerplatztheater	128 Musiker

The München Philharmonic	212 musicians
Orchestra of Radio Station	75 musicians
State Opera	147 musicians
Gärtnerplatztheater	128 musicians

Helmut-Högl-Sextett: 6 Musikanten
6 musicians

In München leben:

28 154 Hunde
36 220 Katzen
 1 379 Pferde
34 369 Hühner
 1 734 Bienenköniginnen
       3 Löwen

Feuerwehr und Polizei fangen jährlich rund 12 entflogene Papageien und retten etwa 40 Enten und Schwäne vor dem Einfrieren.

Numbered among München's residents are:

28,154 dogs
36,220 cats
 1,379 horses
34,369 chickens
 1,734 queen bees
       3 lions

Every year the fire brigade and police force catch some 12 escaped parrots and rescue some 40 ducks and swans that have frozen into the surface of ponds.

Der Stachus ist der verkehrsreichste Platz in Europa. Er wird täglich von

70 000 Autos
50 000 Fußgängern
 3 000 Trambahnen

und einer unbestimmten Anzahl von Hunden über- und unterquert.

The Stachus is Europe's busiest traffic junction. Both above and below ground it is crossed daily by

70,000 cars and trucks
50,000 pedestrians
 3,000 streetcars

and an indeterminate number of dogs.

Caligula heißt diese dressierte Maus.
In einem einzigen Jahr brachte sie ihrem Herrchen
Fritz Sagert:

1 Scheidungsdrohung seiner Gattin
7 Lokalverbote
4 ohnmächtige Frauen

Caligula is the pet-name of this performing mouse.
Over the course of a single year it netted its owner:

1 threat of divorce from his wife
7 blackballings by restaurant proprietors
4 dead faints

ry

seietie

hätsät

In München muß man's phonetisch schreiben, denn man kann's hier nur in Anführung gebrauchen:
Die Stadt zeigte noch nie »Gesellschaft«, denn wer zu ihr gehört, wirklich von Bildung, hohem Können und großem Namen, der geht nicht aus oder nur ganz intim. Das andere, das von zwei männlichen und einer weiblichen Klatschtante durch die Spalten der Boulevardzeitungen gejagt wird, ist eben »soseietie & tschätsät«, deren Bosse (links) ein grimmiges Leben führen, um der heiteren Jugend (oben) fröhliche Spielstunden zu bereiten ...

Words like "society" and "jet-set" are so alien to München that they have to be written phonetically.
"Society life" is something which München has never known, for it has never been the custom of Münchners of rank, achievement or education to "meet out." At most they wine and dine privately in a small intimate circle. The snobriety so effusively celebrated in their columns by München's two pocket-size Walter Winchells and one pocket-size Hedda Hopper falls under the heading of "soseietie & tschätsät," while publicans (left) have to keep their nose to the grindstone in order to provide amusement for the

Vornehm...

Auf der Bühne spielt man's,
im Parkett da ist man's!
(Links: Primaballerina Margot Werner und Kritiker
Maurus Pacher bei einer Faschingsaufführung von
Schwanensee. Rechts: Abendzeitungsherausgeberin
Anneliese Friedmann bei einem Empfang im Bayerischen
Hof.)

Distingué

Those on the stage act distinguished,
those in the orchestra stalls really are distinguished.
(Left: Prima ballerina Margot Werner with critic Maurus
Pacher giving a comic performance of Swan Lake during
Fasching.
Right: Anneliese Friedmann, publisher of the local
Abendzeitung, at a reception in the "Bayerische Hof" –
Hotel.

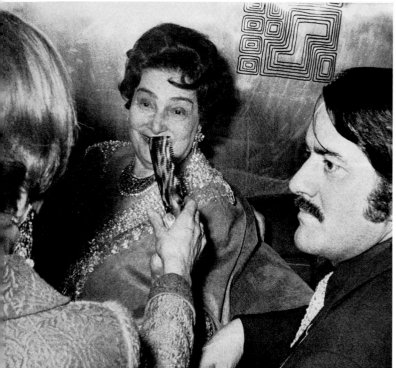

Atemberaubend...
für Chrysanthemenballvorstand Ilse Schrader-Zöllner,
wenn sie Landesvater Goppel zur Polonaise führen darf...

Atemberaubend...
für Schauspieler Nino Korda der Kammaustausch bei
»Diamantenwally« Ysabel Styler selig, über Kaviar und
Chapagner hinweg...

Atemberaubend...
für Minister Schedl die Ablenkung vom anstrengenden
Dienst fürs bayrische Volk...

Breathless...
Ilse Schrader-Zöllner, organizer of the Chrysanthemum
Ball, invited by Minister-President Goppel to a
polonaise...

Breathless...
actor Nino Korda, handing a comb to ''Diamond Wally''
Ysabel Styler across a table of caviar and champagne...

Breathless...
Minister Schedl, finding distraction from strenuous
paperwork in the service of the State of Bavaria...

»äktschn« — oder wie sich die internationalen Gäste bei einem Tanzturnier, Gunter Sachs' Geburtstagshappening oder einem »römischen Thermenfest« auszudrücken pflegen: action!

Action kann in München ein 50-Kubikmeter-Geburtstagsschaumkuchen sein (vom extra dafür eingeflogenen französischen Pop-Künstler César gebacken), auf dem sich 250 »Namen« bis zum

klitschnassen Smokinghemd austoben.—
Action kann aber auch der alte Trick mit dem Swimming-pool-Reinfall sein, sofern alle bis auf das nasse Opfer wissen, wer der

"Action" may mean anything from ballroom dancing contests, a Gunther Sachs Birthday Happening to a Roman Bath Party.
"Action" in München is likely to be an 1800 cubic feet foam birthday cake flown in by French Pop artist César for 250 minor social celebrities to roll over in their sweat-drenched party shirts.
"Action" can also be that hoary stunt of pushing someone into the swimming pool fully clothed. All except the victim know who did the pushing — and was paid a thousand for his services . . .
(Lotti Ohnesorge and Samy Drechsel at the back are still keeping mum about this.)

»Schubser« ist, und daß er einen Tausender dafür kassierte . . .
(auch Lotti Ohnesorge und Samy Drechsel dahinter schweigen darüber bis heute!)

äktschn

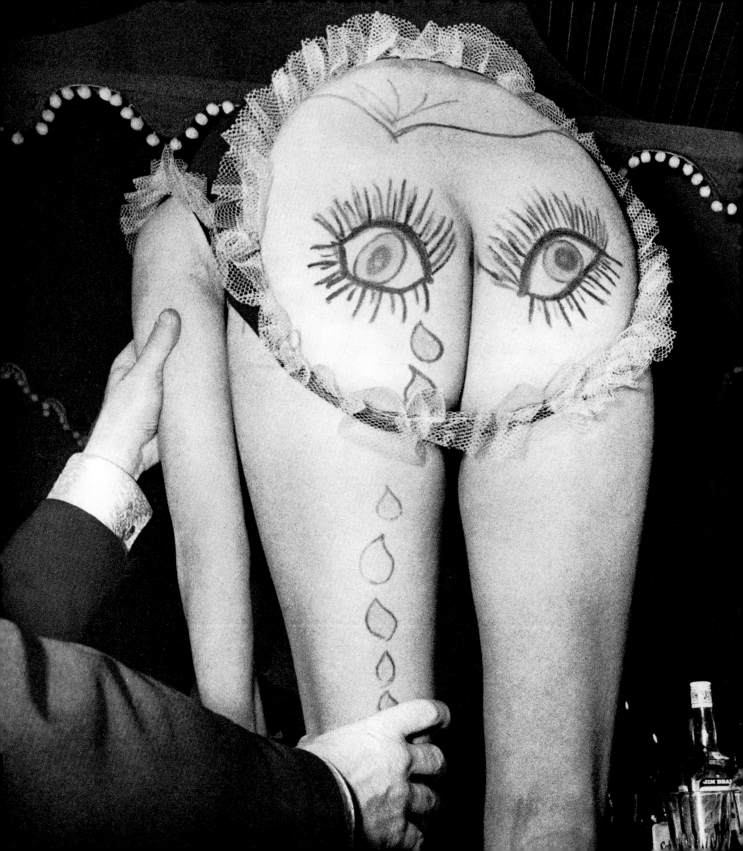

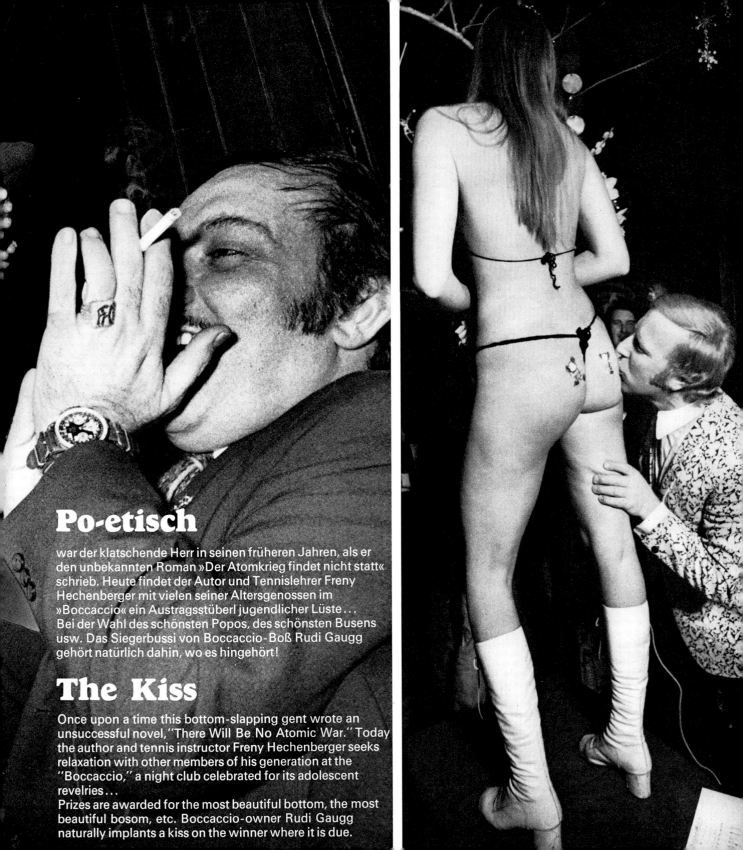

Po-etisch

war der klatschende Herr in seinen früheren Jahren, als er den unbekannten Roman »Der Atomkrieg findet nicht statt« schrieb. Heute findet der Autor und Tennislehrer Freny Hechenberger mit vielen seiner Altersgenossen im »Boccaccio« ein Austragsstüberl jugendlicher Lüste… Bei der Wahl des schönsten Popos, des schönsten Busens usw. Das Siegerbussi von Boccaccio-Boß Rudi Gaugg gehört natürlich dahin, wo es hingehört!

The Kiss

Once upon a time this bottom-slapping gent wrote an unsuccessful novel, "There Will Be No Atomic War." Today the author and tennis instructor Freny Hechenberger seeks relaxation with other members of his generation at the "Boccaccio," a night club celebrated for its adolescent revelries…
Prizes are awarded for the most beautiful bottom, the most beautiful bosom, etc. Boccaccio-owner Rudi Gaugg naturally implants a kiss on the winner where it is due.

Joseph Michael Heger, Pressechef des Rathauses, erfand den Einhandteller für den »homo partyniensis«, den berufsmäßigen Partygeher, der besonders bei anstrengenden offiziellen Stehpartys beim Imbißbalancieren in höchste Schwierigkeiten kommt, wenn er den eigentlichen Zweck solcher Zusammenkünfte erfüllen soll: Handshake und wichtige Konversation!

(Übrigens: Interessierte Fabrikanten für die serienmäßige Herstellung des Partytellers mögen sich bei der Pressestelle des Rathauses, Telefon 2151, anmelden.)

Joseph Michael Heger, Public Relations Chief at City Hall, invented the one-hand plate for homo partyniensis, the professional partygoer who invariably gets into difficulties trying to balance a plate of food in one hand and greet guests with the other while at the same time attempting to keep up a stream of lively small-talk.

(Note: Manufacturers interested in mass producing the party plate should ring the Public Relations Department at City Hall under the number 2151.)

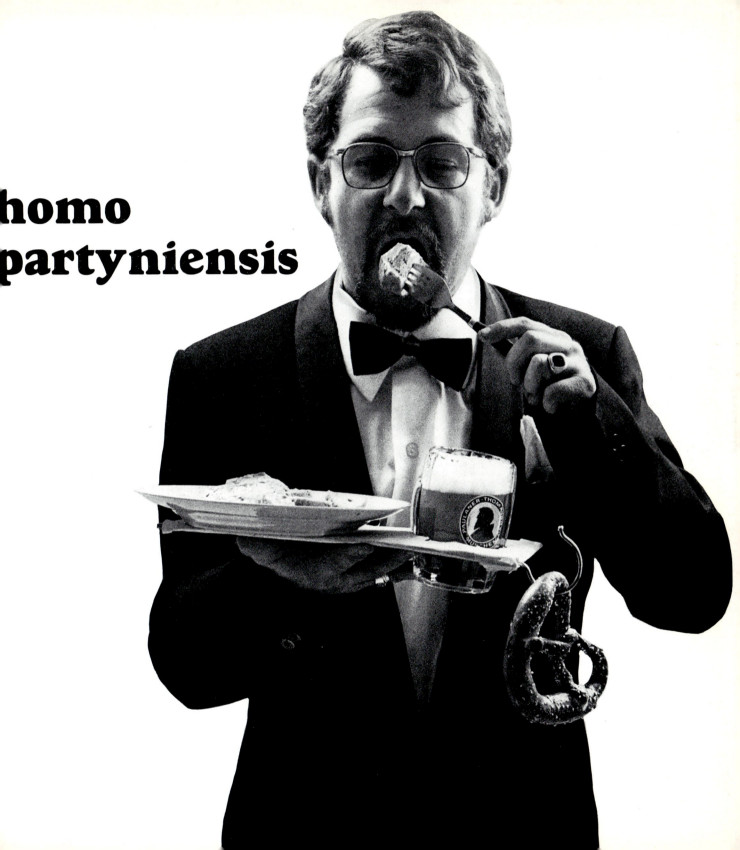

homo
partyniensis

Monika A. (18): Debütantin... Monika A. (18): Deb...

Monika B. (18): Udo-Fan...   Monika B. (18): Rooting for Udo Jürgens...

Monika C. (18): Typ.   Monika C. (18): Hippie...

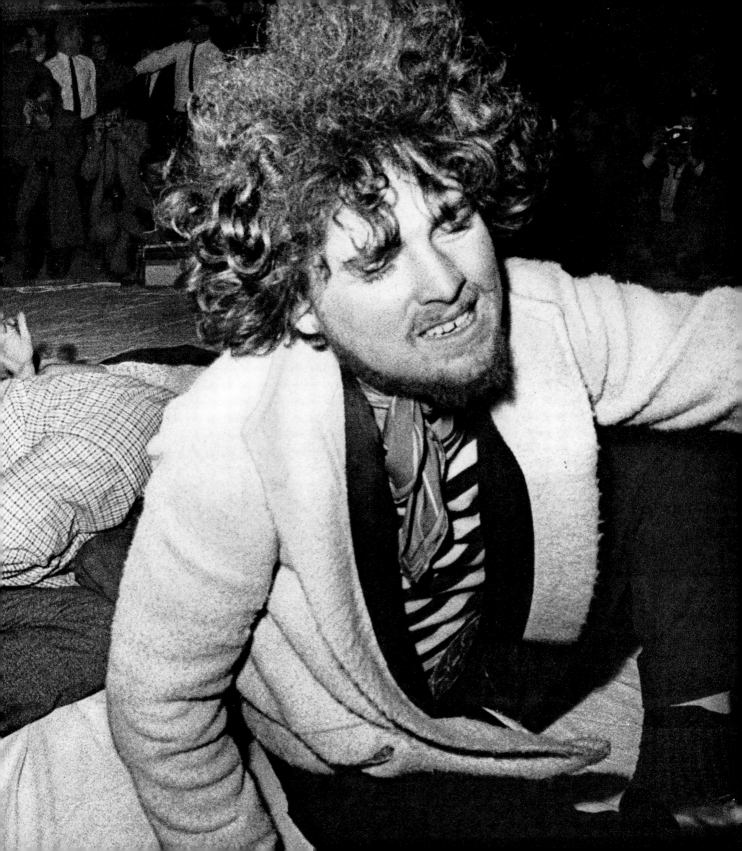

Künstler Artists...

Geister . . . am hellichten Tag!
Ich seh' schwarz!
Doch die vier Musensöhne eines
modernen Theaters kündigen nur
ihr Stück an. Es hieß: »Ja, ja!«

Spooks . . . in broad daylight!
Don't panic – they're only four members
of a modern theater group adver-
tising a new production. This one is
called ''Ja, ja!''

Die sieben Münchner

(nicht die sieben Schwaben) tragen eine wertvolle
Last: Den Maibaum des Hofbräuhauses ...

The Seven Münchners

(not to be confused with The Seven Suabians)
transporting a most precious load: a Maypole
hijacked from the Hofbräuhaus ...

Im Millionendorf

haben sich bäuerliche Bräuche gehalten, wie
zum Beispiel das Maibaumstehlen. Es geht nach genauen
Regeln vor sich. Diese Burschen haben den Baum vom
reichsten Münchner Wirt entführt. Gegen einen ganzen
Banzen Freibier wird er im Triumphzug vierspännig
wieder heimgeführt ins Hofbräuhaus, Münchens
Sehenswürdigkeit Nr. 1!

A village metropolis

Among the time-honored rural customs which still
survive is the hijacking of the Maypole. Would-be
hijackers have to adhere to strict rules of procedure.
These young men succeeded in stealing the Maypole
from München's wealthiest restaurantier, who had to
buy it back at the cost of a barrel of beer. Here the pole
is being borne back in triumph to München's
internationally famous Hofbräuhaus.

Ostern...

verirrte sich einst ein Osterhase auf den Stachus, baute viele kleine Nester, legte Eier und sich selbst hinein.

(Was die schlauen Werbeleute aber nicht bedachten: Daß Turgut Mühüftülüz, links, schon in Istanbul keine Schokoladenhasen leiden konnte!)

At Easter

One day an Easter bunny lost her way at the Stachus, built a lot of little nests and filled them with eggs and herself.

(What the smart publicity boys overlooked was that even back home in Istanbul, Turgut Mühüftülüz (left) never did like chocolate bunnies.)

Prost Abitur!

Nicht aus Schulraumnot, sondern aus »Wir sind ja gar nicht so!« verlegten die Professoren des »Königlich Bayrischen Theresiengymnasiums« die Verleihung der Reifezeugnisse ins »Königlich Bayrische Hofbräuhaus«. Seitdem ist der Königlich Bayrische Trinkspruch erweitert: 1-2-3-4-5-6 gsuffa!

Celebrating matriculation

Not for lack of space but to put on a show of liberal-mindedness, the teachers at the "Royal Bavarian Theresiengymnasium" chose the Royal Bavarian Hofbräuhaus as a site for the ritual handing over of matriculation certificates. Ever since, the Royal Bavarian drinking toast has accordingly been extended from eins-zwei-gsuffa to 1-2-3-4-5-6-gsuffa!

1.364.498 Münchner schlafen
Münchners in bed.

1 364 498 Münchner schlafen – 422 sind unterwegs.
Um 4.00 Uhr früh – die moderne Geisterstunde. Auto-
knacker, Penner, Nachtwächter, Polizisten, Striptease-
tänzerinnen auf dem Heimweg, Taxifahrer und die letzte
»Dame«...

When 1,364,498 Münchners are asleep, 422 are abroad.
At 4 a.m. – the hour when modern ghosts walk the streets:
car-pilferers, bums, night watchmen, policemen, striptease
artists on the way home, cab drivers – and the last street-
walker...

Maximilianstraße

Ludwigstraße

Die Kehrseite der Stadt.—
Ein Türke packt's mit Allah,
ein Italiener con dio,
der Dominikanermönch
vor der Theatinerkirche
packt's mit Gott!

The other side of life—
A Turk does his thing
with the help of Allah,
an Italian con dio,
the Dominican friar in front of
the Theatine Church
with God.

Schwabing – Leopoldstraße

„Bullen am Morgen bringen Kummer und Sorgen"

Sie wissen's in Düsseldorf, London und Sidney: Im Englischen Garten kampieren die Typen. Die Polizei weiß es auch und holt sich ein paar, wenn sie sich zu stark vermehren.

Cops

In Düsseldorf, London, Sydney, the word has spread that hippies can pass the night in the English Gardens. Whenever they become too numerous, the police arrive to thin them out.

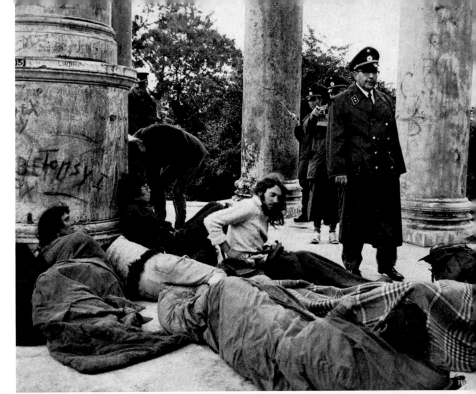

Der Verkehr soll folgendermaßen eingeteilt werden:

7–8 Uhr: Personenautos	11–12 Uhr: die Radfahrer
8–9 Uhr: Geschäftsautos	12–13 Uhr: Omnibusse
9–10 Uhr: Straßenbahnen	13–14 Uhr: die Fußgänger
10–11 Uhr: die Feuerwehr	

Sollte diese stundenweise Einteilung nicht möglich sein, so gäbe es eine andere Lösung, und zwar Tagesverkehr:

Montag:	Personenautos	Donnerstag:	Omnibusse
Dienstag:	Geschäftsautos	Freitag:	die Feuerwehr
Mittwoch:	Straßenbahnen	Samstag:	die Radfahrer

Die Sonn- und Feiertage sind nur für die Fußgänger. Auf diese Weise würde nie wieder ein Mensch überfahren werden.

Oder eine weitere Lösung:
Im 20. Jahrhundert: Personenautos
Im 21. Jahrhundert: Geschäftsautos
Im 22. Jahrhundert...

(Dieser 1939 von dem Münchner Bürger Valentin Fey -alias Karl Valentin - vorgebrachte Vorschlag zur Verbesserung der Verkehrslage an der Isar wurde bis heute nicht verwirklicht.)

The various classes of traffic will observe the following timetable:

07–08 Private cars	10–11 Fire engines
08–09 Delivery cars and trucks	11–12 Cyclists
09–10 Streetcars	12–13 Buses
	13–14 Pedestrians

Should this timetable prove impracticable, it could be revised as follows:

Monday	Private cars	Thursday	Buses
Tuesday	Delivery cars and trucks	Friday	Fire engines
Wednesday	Streetcars	Saturday	Cyclists

Sundays and public holidays to be reserved for pedestrians. The implementation of this scheme would assure that no pedestrians would ever be run over.

Or another solution:

20th century	Private cars
21st century	Delivery cars and trucks
22nd century...	

(This scheme for the improvement of traffic conditions proposed by München Citizen Valentin Fey, alias Karl Valentin, in 1939 has not as yet been introduced.)

Verkehrsprobleme

gibt es 32 Jahre später wiederum nur für Leute ohne Ideen!

Transport problems

exist – 32 years later – only for people who lack inventive genius.

Kriminalrat Georg Schmid: »Zum Glück sind wir in München so weit, daß sich ein Polizist einem Demonstranten unterhaken kann und ihn auf so persönliche Art zum Weitergehen auffordert!«

CID official Georg Schmid: "In München we have fortunately matured to the point where a police officer can link arms with a demonstrator in a friendly fashion and so keep everything on the move."

Die Vergangenheit wird in München
aufbewahrt im:

Stadtmuseum
Völkerkundemuseum
Nationalmuseum
Deutschen Museum
Theatermuseum
Residenzmuseum
Jagdmuseum
Brauereimuseum
und im Valentin-Musäum.

Geöffnet von 11.01 bis 17.29 Uhr.
99jährige in Begleitung ihrer Eltern haben
freien Eintritt, sonst 99 Pfennige.

Wo?
Im Isartor-Turm, von den Raubrittern und
U-Bahn-Erbauern bis heute verschont.

Was?
Drei Stockwerke Staunen über die liebe-
voll gesammelten Erinnerungen an den
größten Münchner Komiker: Karl Valentin.

Ein Unikum aus diesen längst vergange-
nen Tagen, der Peps, bewacht das
Musäum für unwiederbringlichen Humor.

München's past is kept stored at:

Stadtmuseum
Völkerkundemuseum
Nationalmuseum
Deutsches Museum
Theatermuseum
Residenzmuseum
Jagdmuseum
Brauereimuseum
and the Valentin Museum

Visiting hours from 11.01 to 17.29.
Persons in their 99th year are entitled to
free admission if accompanied by their
parents. Otherwise the charge is
99 pfennigs.

Where?
The Isartor Tower, still intact to this day,
despite robber-knights and subway
constructors.
What?
Three floors of amusement and surprise
at the fondly collected souvenirs
commemorating München's greatest
humorist: Karl Valentin.

Peps, a character from byegone days,
guards this "museum for irrecoverable
humor".

„Kasimir, wir folgen Dir!"

Wenn in München der Fasching* ausgebrochen ist, stürzen sich die Ur-Ur-Ahnen der mittelalterlichen Raub-ritter, die »damischen Ritter«, mit Mann, Roß und Bier in die Saalschlachten…
*(nicht zu verwechseln oder gar gleichzusetzen mit »Karneval«).

"Once more into the breach, Casimir!"

When Fasching* breaks out in München, the Crazy Knights, great-great-great-grandfathers of the medieval Robber-Knights, join the affray with chargers and beer…
(*Not to be confused or equated with "carnival.")

Oberbürgermeister Dr. Vogel
Chief Burgomaster Dr. Vogel

Während es den »konservativen« Münchnern Spaß macht, sich nach alter Sitte im Fasching zu verkleiden...

Playboy James Graser

Stadtpfarrer Max Zistl
City Clergyman Max Zistl

Whereas members of München's Establishment delight in the old Fasching custom of putting on disguise...

Schauspieler Hans Clarin
Actor Hans Clarin

Schauspielerin Andrea Rau
Actress Andrea Rau

Stadträtin Ria Burgard
City Counsellor Ria Burgard

...halten die »Fortschrittlichen«
eher das Gegenteil für richtig.

...the more progressive
prefer the opposite.

Waldi der Exilmünchner

Millionenfach geht er um die Welt als Maskottche[n]
für die Olympischen Spiele in München. Der Orig[inal]
Waldi aber, ein urbayrischer Rauhhaardackel, lebt [im]
»Exil« in Paris bei Felix Levitan, dem Präsidenten d[er]
Internationalen Sportpresse.
Nur manchmal, beim Blick auf die Seine, bekomm[t]
er Heimweh zur Isar, aber ein Dackel weint nicht,
er bellt!

Waldi, the Münchner in exi[le]

Millions like him are to be found all over the world [as]
souvenirs of the München Olympics. The original
Waldi, a true Bavarian wire-hair dachshund, lives i[n]
''exile'' at the Paris home of Felix Levitan, Presiden[t]
of International Sport Relations. Only when starin[g at]
the Seine does he occasionally feel nostalgia for th[e]
Isar. But a genuine dachshund does not whine; he
barks his head off.

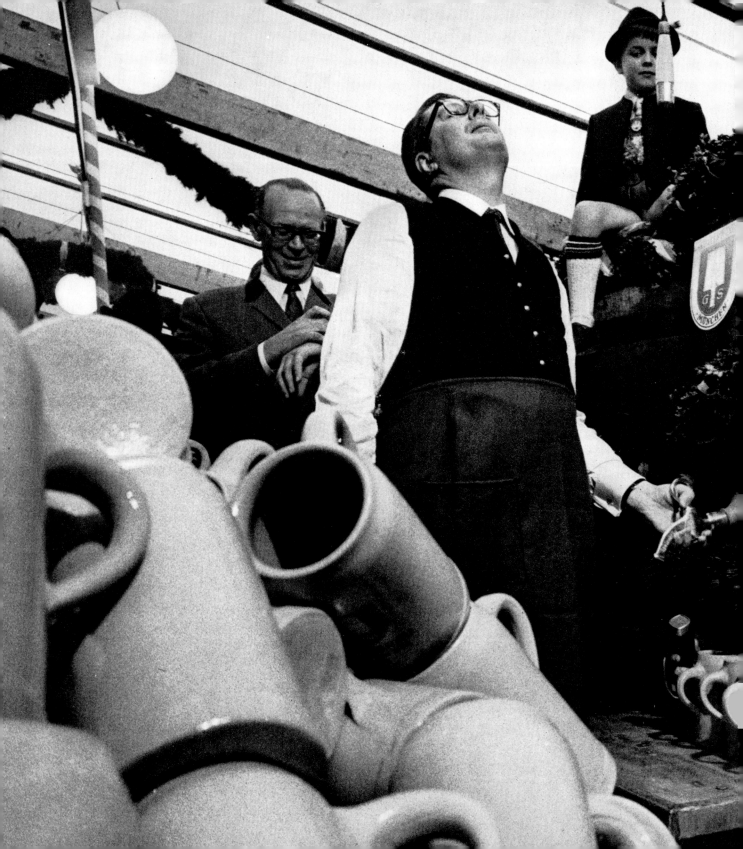

Hansis Stoßgebet

»Gib mir weiterhin das letzte Wort und dem Stadtrat Schmid keine rechten Argumente, gib, daß der Zimniok, der Schlangenzüchter, endlich ans Licht komme mit seinen U-Bahn-Wühlmäusen, gib, daß das Olympiadorf nicht sündig und teuer werde und daß nicht noch viele andere wie der Mönch Timofey ihre Hütten auf dem Oberwiesenfeld bauen. Gib, daß wir auch im weißen Kreis so rot bleiben, ganz ohne revolutionären Elan wie bisher. Gib den Studenten ein glattes Kinn und eine blanke Stirn, wie ich sie Dir entgegenhebe, und last not least, gib, daß es nicht spritzt, wenn ich wieder ein Faß aufmache zur höheren Ehre der Münchner Stadt!«

Hansi's fervent prayer

All other qualifications of München's Chief Burgomaster are of small account as compared to his ability to knock the broaching tap into a barrel of beer at the Oktoberfest with a single blow. If he fails in this, his fellow citizens will consider him a very wet rag — and not only as regards beer. So he has good reason to look prayerful.

Peter Alexander

Heinz Gebhardt

Heinz Gebhardt, Jahrgang 1947 und in München geboren, ist Fotograf aus Leidenschaft: Er war kaum vierzehnjährig, als sein erstes Foto im »Münchner Merkur« veröffentlicht wurde. Auf dem von ihm geschossenen Zielfoto eines Radrenn-Länderkampfes ging eindeutig ein anderer als Sieger hervor, als vom Kampfgericht entschieden worden war.
Während seiner Gymnasiumszeit verdiente sich Heinz Gebhardt als Sportfotograf die ersten eigenen Kameras. Nach der mittleren Reife besuchte er zwei Jahre die Bayrische Staatslehranstalt für Fotografie. 1968 gewann er den »Europapreis für Foto und Film« der UNESCO. Mit der Kamera hatte er damals bereits dreimal die Türkei und Persien und halb Europa bereist und bei der Olympiade in Mexiko fotografiert.
Von 1968 an spielte Gebhardt für die damals neu gegründete Boulevardzeitung »tz« den »rasenden Fotoreporter«, später arbeitete er für die »Abendzeitung« und die Illustrierte »Quick«. Seit vergangenem Jahr lebt Heinz Gebhardt als freier Fotograf in München.

Heinz Gebhardt, born in 1947 in München, a passionate photographer, was barely fourteen when his first photograph appeared in the »Münchner Merkur«, a local daily. In this snapshot of the end of an inter-regional bicycle race, the victor was clearly not the one declared as such by the judges.
While still at junior college, Heinz Gebhardt earned the price of his first cameras as a photographer of sporting events. After passing his secondary examinations he attended the Bavarian State Institute of Photography for two years. In 1968 he won the UNESCO European Award for Photography and Film. By then he had already toured Turkey, Persia and half of Europe three times with his camera and had also covered the Mexican Olympics. In 1968 Gebhardt joined München's newly founded tabloid »tz« as a roving photographic reporter, later changing to the »Abendzeitung« and the illustrated weekly »Quick«. Last year he struck out on a new career as a free-lance photographer in München.

Karl Wanninger

Karl Wanninger, Jahrgang 1922, ist geborener Münchner, fühlt sich aber vor allem als echter »Sendlinger«: In der Vorstadt, die bis heute viel mehr als etwa Schwabing ihre münchnerische Eigenart bewahrt hat, ist er aufgewachsen und zur Schule gegangen. Nach Lehrzeit und Krieg besuchte er zunächst eine Sprachenschule und arbeitete dann von 1946 an als Journalist für eine Musikerzeitschrift und als Herausgeber eines Pressedienstes. Von 1946 bis 1968 war er Lokalredakteur beim »Münchner Merkur«, seit 1968 ist er Chef der Lokalredaktion der »tz«, zu deren Gründungsmitgliedern er gehört. Zusammen mit Herbert Schneider schrieb Karl Wanninger das »Münchner Bummelbuch«, daneben gibt es von ihm zahlreiche Veröffentlichungen zu kulinarischen Themen.

Karl Wanninger, although born in München in 1922, considers himself essentially a true native of Sendling, the suburb in which he grew up and went to school, and which still preserves its Münchner character even more than Schwabing. After apprenticeship and the war, he first attended a language school and, in 1946, started as a journalist on a music magazin and became the head of a press agency. From 1946 to 1968 he served as local editor on the »Münchner Merkur« and from 1969 as local editor-in-chief on the »tz«, of which he was one of the founding members. He is co-author with Herbert Schneider of the *Münchner Bummelbuch* and the author of numerous articles on culinary subjects.

Übertragung ins Englische von Michael O'Donnell

English translation by Michael O'Donnell

© 1972 Verlag F. Bruckmann KG, München
Alle Rechte vorbehalten
Herstellung: F. Bruckmann KG, München,
Graphische Kunstanstalten
Printed in Germany
ISBN 3 7654 1450 6